Bright Yellow Buzz

Lee Slonimsky

Spuyten Duyvil
New York City

ISBN 978-1-956005-62-2

Library of Congress Cataloging-in-Publication Data

Names: Slonimsky, Lee, author.
Title: Bright yellow buzz / Lee Slonimsky.
Description: New York City : Spuyten Duyvil, [2022] |
Identifiers: LCCN 2022009803 | ISBN 9781956005622 (paperback)
Subjects: LCGFT: Poetry.
Classification: LCC PS3619.L67 B75 2022 | DDC 811/.6--dc23
LC record available at https://lccn.loc.gov/2022009803

For The Mathematical Abilities Of Bees

CONTENTS

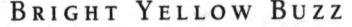

BRIGHT YELLOW BUZZ

INTRODUCTION

> *"Stop! Put easel on this*
> *road!"*

So revered American poet Lee Slonimsky, in *Bright Yellow Buzz*, his tenth collection of master verse, exhorts young Rembrandt ("Young Rembrandt Wanders in Europe"). The poet, in these predominantly recent pieces, wields his words with the sensibility of an artist—truly, artist-poet—in a long landscape where there is the possibility of observing "Immortal leaves" which "never wither" ("Each Cell Has Its Own Clock"), yet is also a place that is as much mortally bound:

> A surer path to immortality
> is that of art; but so infrequently
> ("Rembrandt")

"Infrequently" is fraught; it seems to envision a natural order frail enough to be determined by "surprise" ("The Waiting"), "digression" ("Painted For Free, and Forever Lost Now), and "error's hope" ("As The Year Turns: After L. Zukofsky"), yet imply, at the same time, an ultimate judgment: that of the "value" of "spirit's truth" ("Young Rembrandt Wanders Europe"). As such, transcendent technique is impelled: technique of human creativity, and technique of human fulfillment, which is the subject, the weight, the work, the beauty, of this poetry.

Slonimsky characteristically writes in a compelling, inclusive "you" (never "I"), as with this arresting example from "The Waiting:" "You cannot praise your feebleness!" In so doing the poet formally addresses a living soul, his subject; but with the same word, and the same sense, also addresses, indeed entreats, his reader, and himself. His signature voice is in an intricate present palpable with past. This may be heard in language and setting as subtly, historically, evocative as

A breeze riffles the open pages of

Horace

  ("Exchange Students")

or, often, heard as a more urgent and elegiac voice of misplacement,
of change; indeed, of loss. One watches "a dragonfly's mid-winter
loop" ("As The Year Turns: After L. Zukofsky"); one descends steps
from August, into Autumn, "as if it's summer, just beginning" ("Ice
Age"). There is everywhere in Slonimsky's poetry both mathematical
and artistic precision in the observed, and in the language writing it,
yet it is a precision of paradox, and undefinable pathos; perspective
which is achingly long, yet never long enough:

Now,
we knew the dragonflies would not live long
as individuals, but could respect
three hundred million years
  ("Paleontologists' Vacation")

While an "autumn sense" {"Bird In The Low Lying Branches") is
imbued in these poems, loss is brought to its limits in this collection
in two major works which recount ancient apocalypse, yet are so
much of our own time of inner and outer poverty and contagion. In
"Vesuvius," a well-off idler who, earlier in the day, was "quite struck"
by a different quality of sunlight on his courtyard tiles, must now
abruptly face wrath:

Then, barely noticed, one charred cloud.

What's that?

And, in "Before The Lisbon Earthquake," a relatively youthful piece from 1984, there is, just before catastrophe,

> an eight year old boy
> darting through alleyway shadows
> looking for fruit rolled off a wagon

The poet is clear in his poetry of the cosmos that disaster is not unleashed in nature without warnings (and, implied, judgement). In the case of the Lisbon earthquake, he writes: "many warnings were given," and, most memorably, "children spat up blood as they dreamed of ruins." Yet the end comes in chillingly straightforward lines:

> On the day the earthquake came,
> there was no warning at all

"Before The Lisbon Earthquake" also appears in this collection in a recent Greek translation by Greece's State Literary Award winner Stamatis Polenakis, who has also translated Slonimsky's 2007 volume *Pythagoras in Love*. (Notable French and Polish translations of that work are also available.)

Slonimsky, an authority in all things sonnet, continues to offer in *Bright Yellow Buzz* the apotheosis of modern sonnet form: the reader is pulsed irretrievably into image, narrative, and meditation in phrase and line as formally fluent as is allowed by the English language. Slonimsky, a mentor to many of today's notable poets, has also included in this new collection free verse pieces, haiku, and triolet along with the sonnets. His mastery of language has always been in finding nature's prosody: sometimes sumptuous, sometimes somber, rhyme is in the rhythm, and rhythm in the rhyme, as: "a nature miniature" ("Vermeer Near Tupper Lake"), and: "a fluent flutery" ("The Infinite"). Here, as ever, is writing as a metaphoric blending of the poet's observation, of mathematics, of painterly depiction, of sound syllabic; it is often unabashedly beautiful iambic pentameter:

> July's seethe-heart; the subtleties of sear
> and sizzle sifted through leaves' lushery."
> ("Submission in August")

Yet even where such favored, elegant meter pervades, stresses sway and shift, as line lengthens or contracts in the expression of image and meaning: even when the assonance and consonance of the words and the rhythms are not apparent to the eye, they are to the ear, as the phrased line slows and speeds, and spondee, trochee, anapest emerge:

> Falling snow's replaced by blue sky; a few clouds
> become artistes. They grace bare slopes with feathers,
> slivers, blooms as round as late spring flowers;
> no-one could forget their sculptures.

> Seeds
> for you, remembering years later in
> your shabby Paris studio. And yet,
> despite cloudart, your mountainscape seems wan,
> without the vivid freshness of surprise
> that day, post-storm.
> ("The Waiting")

And, even well-travelled meter is at one with hyper-modernity of imaging in this poetry; thus, from "Green:"

And no real gap between branches, his bones

and, from "Still:"

Cicadashrill smoothes into autumn's Slow
while leaves that dry and start to tatter

      sing

While phrases in a Slonimsky poem of any form suffuse in assured assonance, and consonance, he is readily recognizable on the page by the compounded word. Such word compounding, seen, for example, in the above verse from "The Waiting," "Still," and "Glaze;" in "branchsharp shadows" ("Summer School"), and, perhaps most beautifully of all, in these:

at beakshape, wingfluff, any resemblance
that might inspire recognition

          ("Antidote")

as if one sunray has soaked this leaf
amidst loudsweet waters

          ("Glaze")

is in inspired kinship with Hopkins, and Celan, and with Slonimsky's own honored and long-time mentor, colleague, and friend, former Consultant in Poetry to the Library of Congress Daniel Hoffman.

In Slonimsky's poetry, a uniquely pitched and deeply drawn anthropomorphic vision inheres; vivid and existentially animated images abound. Here, an oak tree is not only in voice, but is "neurasthenic;" here, gnats "banish winter where it really matters;" here, there is "gust-loved leaf." Most arrestingly, in "Before the Lisbon Earthquake," there are boulders "forming letters in every known language, spelling out imminent doom;" there are rocks that "duplicated what was coming, splitting to bits without ready cause, imitating earthquake's pure chaos." Such anthropomorphism is, in fact, exquisite meditation on the provenance of the living spirit, may be discerned in

past life

or verve
("Ancestors")

and is sustaining, even celebratory, even when it remains only meditation: "His story's blurred before Pythagoras, but each ancestor's treasured all the same" ("Ancestors").

As reflected in the above quoted series of Rembrandt poems, this new collection accrues vivid painterly obsession and manner, as must be, to attend to "Potentates of pause and poise, and pose" ("A Painter Begins"). Such poems arc specific exhortation, and exaltation, of the artist-poet who, striving in "reason's instability" ("Macbeth's Castle: Philosophers' Woods"), may "multiply sweet nature by pure light" ("The Waiting") in the plein-air of "patron" nature ("Young Rembrandt Wanders Europe"). Such exaltation is at apogee in "Vermeer Near Tupper Lake:" even "gold petal etchings," which "amaze" as craftsmanship of nature, are seen as "Vermeer of the precise." Truly, Slonimsky's evolving finesse in portraying the pictorial artist, at one with poet, philosopher, and nature itself, in exegesis of an infinite landscape, is a glory of this collection and, particularly in the simultaneous observation of the artistry of nature itself, much a matter of faith. The artist-poet is allowed "some nature oils" ("Painted For Free, and Forever Lost Now"), but of human creativity and human fulfillment thereof, Slonimsky has his own verdict:

but something more's required than technique,
and memory

("The Waiting")

The poems in this new collection remain under the daunting mastery of the figure out of Samos, Pythagoras: mathematics still is ascendant, central to a life of observation of the nature of things, the renderings of the art of it:

> the indivisible numbers that
> are true immortals, irreversibly whole
> as gods should be
>
> ("Bird, Flower, Waves")

Yet, there is also a knowingness, and a reaching, beyond this; Slonimsky, at times strikingly Yeatsian, as in his "need for colloquy to make thoughts whole" ("The Athens Academy") now, as poet, as artist, as Pythagoras himself, "ponders." Now, consideration of what has been empiric "Depends on my mood" ("Field Trips, Athens, 202 B.C.). Indeed, as the poet nears seventy, there seems more and more urgency and elegy in reaching to reconcile the diversities, even paradoxes, among loss, longing, natural beauty and being, mathematics, logic, and creation. Such reconciliation is reflected, even celebrated, in the collection's title, taken from "The Neurasthenic Oak Tree," posing not only bees as harbingers of nature's spring, but natural order itself as the work of a "fragranter," a "flowerer," anchored in primes (this is reinforced by the collection's dedication, "For The Mathematical Abilities Of Bees"). And if a tense irony may be read in the reconciliation, it is, in part, because

> when fresh wind stirs
> the raindrops' perfect circles elongate;
> distort; in ways he cannot calculate
>
> ("Challenge Of The Wind").

Lee Slonimsky's poetic achievement in *Bright Yellow Buzz* is more than technique, more than memory, though master technique and master memory are everywhere in this work: it is nothing less than "spirit's truth;" nothing less than transport: his landscape is written as though pen touched on bough. The artist-poet weathers in the work, in nature's unknowable, even as comprehensive "truth" may prove illusory:

> Deep Scottish truth seems well beyond our reach,
>   obscured by shadows we can never breach
>   ("Macbeth's Castle: Philosophers' Woods").

And if the urgency of artistic creation and human fulfillment must finally fall away, and even its elegy lost, still, essential, if spare, solace remains:

> this could be
> how it ends.
>
> darker than the absence of light
> but not as cold as might
> be expected
>   ("Blue Sky Bask")

Some seek immortality; some, no more than blessing. Both may be found in these irreplaceable pages.

Robert C. Basner,
September 23rd 2021

Vesuvius

He had that very morning been quite struck
by sunlight on his courtyard tiles; by how
the light appeared to have a quality
he'd never seen before. A gauzy look,
weblike, *as if imprisoning.*

Allow

for his own dreaminess, he still could see
this light was different. It made red tiles glow,
as if they surged from bubbling fire below.

The tiles enclosed a shallow, pale blue pool
that shimmered with the rising sun's hot rays;
he lingered with this lightshow—radiant—
for hours, did no work. Lost in a maze
of brightness, shadow; a pawn of weather's rule.

Then, barely noticed, one charred cloud.

What's that?

Vermeer Near Tupper Lake

A delicate gold figure, lightly traced
upon a wan white petal. Looks just like
an open scroll, perched on a music stand.

A *nature-miniature*. You pause to look,
amazed by craftsmanship. As if you've found
Vermeer of the precise. What wonders never cease
in woods' gustblown, deep repertoire. How does
this flower know a scroll, an orchestra?

The pattern's present on more petals. Wild,
the way they form a school of art! Beebuzz,
larkchirp, do they read music from
gold petal etchings?

                      Summer chorus lilts
soft air around the flowers; breezed leaves hum
a background. Hummingbird's wings whir.

Young Rembrandt Wanders Europe

reader's note: In regard to this painting poem and the ones that follow it, only those poems specifically mentioning Rembrandt refer to him.

Ineffable fluff—not measurable—but bright
as gleam of dawn itself. This cloud shaped mist,
as beautiful as water, windy air,
would be your perfect painting, if one could exist.

You're trained in portraiture but might you dare
portray this hilltop veil enhanced by light?
But who would be your patron, Nature? *Lord
Well-Wrinkled Earth* (a modest vanity
that hungers for Art's immortality)?

Your payment...of the spirit!

                        You were bored,
no doubt, with Amsterdam society,
and sunsoaked cloudscape might just liberate
from frill and shrill.

                  Stop! Put easel on this road!
Your spirit's truth: and there's no way to calculate
its value amidst such sharp and brilliant light.

Painted For Free, And Forever Lost Now

A wisp of sunsoaked cloud is in the bowl
of blue between two rounded hills deep green
with August's tangled leafery. This scene
inspires Rembrandt. In his studio
he has some "nature oils." It's best to fill
his thoughts with cloud's details, paint on return;
and add to the digression he loves so.

A face engages still now, but he yearns
at some great inner depth to capture light
in perfect interplay with morning's mist,
bright leaves and hillshaped round. Frail streak of cloud
assumes a subject's qualities.

                         He'll brood
on every breeze-twirled nuance in his sight,
until he's back. Art's air! He must exist.

Black Branch, Gold Sun Ray

Late February woods *quintessence* sparse,
the loftiest bare branches delicate
as sunlight-polished rapiers fencing with
blue gusts, cloud puffs.

                         You try to calculate
such winter emptiness, austere yet smooth,
contrasted with the coming green. Immerse
yourself in purest numbers of deep May.
But math is smalled by beauty: you'd prefer
to sketch or sculpt, not count.

                             Not easy, though
to capture branch-etched windy air, or whir
of red streaked wings with paint. Your true love's *Slow,*
that's best expressed with quiet, near-still art.

You chose the wrong career: you hear your heart!
You'll start by drawing black branch, gold sun ray.

THE WAITING

Falling snow's replaced by blue sky; clouds
become *artistes*. They grace bare slopes with feathers,
slivers, blooms as round as late spring flowers;
no-one could forget their sculptures.

                                 Seeds
for you, remembering years later in
your shabby Paris studio. And yet,
despite cloudart, your mountainscape seems wan,
without the vivid freshness of surprise
that day, post-storm. Seems *lacking*. You can't praise
your feebleness!

                     White curlicues of mist
decreed, back then, the artist's life your fate,
but if you can't recapture...

                              Art exists,
it seems, to multiply sweet nature by pure light;
but something more's required than technique;
and memory. Despair creeps in.

                            Morose, you wait.

ARTIST AS MAGICIAN

This ball of glimmer, cloud of sunstruck mist,
so low in the air it dances on tree crowns;
this ballerina of smooth roll and bounce,
is just the reason that his art exists.

But how to capture motion with mere paint?
Evoke each cloudball's drift, shimmy and feint?

Technique's the answer, naturally. He's long
at his easel now, today, eliciting
a sense of *move* from daub and stroke. The dance
of cloudpuff, wind-urged, just above the trees.
Lithe mist that loves sunlight and steady breeze.

His concentration turns into a trance:
at last he's mastered leaves' perspective and
twirl's visible!

                    As if he's waved a wand.

A Painter Begins

Clouds must be acrobats
to perch like this on hillside treetops
in first morning light.

Potentates of pause and poise,
and pose:
silver mists revered
by leaves' dew-radiant calm lushery.

They draw the artist's eye,
lingering until

a penciled sketch is done.

The Challenge

He has an inspiration: to convey
that moment in late August when a chill
announces that the summer cannot stay.

The omen's in a brisk late morning breeze,
and manifests in certain subtle ways:
a slightly dimmer light; some slowing birds;
a lesser green. Branch sag.

                  But paint's not words;
he has the will, but can he find details?

He's felt beleaguered lately: no acclaim
or sales. This forest scene, "The Seasons," can
be quite decisive, let him make a name
in London, Paris.

                But that sense of *change*—

in what goes on the canvas, not in woods,
eludes his skill. He spends a grueling day
without one daub to start him on his way.

SUBMISSION IN AUGUST

A sense of summer dwindles everywhere:
in longer shadows, evening chill, a sharp
cool breeze near noon at times. But he must paint
July's *seethe-heart*; the subtleties of sear
and sizzle sifted through leaves' lushery.
Since that's his goal no matter what the length
of time it takes.

                       Fall may come blustery,
but *will* is all. Submission to his Art.

The wind has knocked his easel down today,
and more than once. *So* scattered paints, he weeps
frustratedly.

                      Late August will not sway
him from his mission though—sunlight on leaves—
the torrid challenge in which he believes
so much, he's hot! No matter cold gusts' rips.

GRADUATION

A challenge, yes, to capture how they perch:
low clouds upon lush treetops late in May.
As if they're odd fog-flowers, blooms of mist.
Quite fleeting, so his theme's precarious.
He struggles with some nuances, can't say
if he needs a new mentor who can teach
how light highlights cloud-poise, the pose of mist.

A painter has to learn, not just exist.

He'd thought of Switzerland as school and now
he should be mastering these English hills;
slow drear of morning fog; then sun; thick trees.

He's dreamed himself a genius, *past* degrees
from fine arts schools, or famous names. The thrills

of pure applause, acclaim:

                                    but nothing flows.

Summer School

Sunlight instructs in many angles when
you're in the woods, midmorning. Glance about.

Rays' geometric lessons can begin.

Sunlight instructs in many angles when
the sky is cloudless. What a teacher, sun.
Its branchsharp shadows etch with deep math's wit.

Sunlight instructs in many angles when
you're in the woods, midmorning. Glance about.

REMBRANDT

Methuselah's quaint methodology
was once to mime the slowness of a tree
in motion, worry: *cellish* green blood pace.

Not treat this life as such a dizzying race,
or sprawl of stress.

                To snooze, to laze, to gaze
at leafy branches in a city park,
to have the psyche of a tranquil breeze
and be to anger as; sunlight to dark;

can percolate extreme longevity.

And so it did sometimes; but tragically
the patientest could still slip into haste;
fall prey to accidents without a trace.

A surer path toward immortality
is that of art: but so infrequently.

THE MOVIE STAR

The face of wither is this fading flower,
once purple in the sunshine but now wan
beneath a drizzly sky. Its petals frayed
as if they might be in their final hour.

Old purple beauty's lost without the sun,
and soon come gales to chill, and rip, and tatter,
without remorse for what they have destroyed.

The world of weather knows no guilt or sin.

There's beauty, though, in pale and poignant ruin,
when sun returns. A single petal still
can shine, with startling tints, in the right light,
(though torn).

                Much like a star afraid to fail
in late career, who manages the bright
fate of acclaim. Then lingers on her throne.

THE PRECIPICE

This meeting of the blue math faculty,
assembly of most learned chicories,
takes place late August at semester's edge.
All use an outdoor room of sun and breeze,
bush-boundaried well up on a wooded ridge;
compose prime-number-petaled syllabi
that will instruct in sums and ratios.

Amazing, what a single flower knows!

Their dialogue's more somber, though, this year;
soft petal murmuring breeze evokes pale gray;
a threat looms to their university.
Nearby new-ski-slope clearing drives a fear
of study's end. Of vanished colloquy.

What would be learning then, no-one can say.

What Silence

September's an assassin, this strange year:
your friends the chicories have not survived!
Past midnight August thirty first, they're gone.

Next morning, walking, full of loss and fear,
you wonder *what* it was. Some gusts that scythed?
An unrecorded chill? This dreary, sodden dawn
reveals a startling, striking emptiness
that devastates. Sweet summer laid to rest.

Their math was quite fantastic, these savants who taught
prime number ratios with petal-counts;
yet fall's first victims, now. Colleagues; mentors too.
Their lustrous deep blue knew far more than you,
and oh, what silence. All you can do is wait
for greenbright May; blue memories will haunt.

BEAUTY, TRUTH

A *flowerer*'s real challenge is in math,
interpreting prime number petal counts
among the chicories. Their sequences.
Or finding ratios between the tints
of pink and red in roses.

                      On his path
this sunslashed morning, he can see at least
four number riddles to unravel. Now
he'll conquer them, as deep math skills allow.

But making flowers numbers doesn't quite
fulfill his instincts for their beauty, truth.
He longs for more: perhaps to meditate
on how their hues distill rainbows, sunlight;
a shimmer that he'll never calculate.
He longs to be more than savant of math.

Sun Flowers By Ginger F. Zaimis

When the sun tones dark—
And you forage trepid; inward
With whom do you speak, Lark?

No Buzz From Bees

It's onerous at times, his self-assigned
vocation as a flowerer. The math's
relentless in its obligations. No
diversion with mere fragrance or allure;
a flower's life is number at the core;
now petal-count, then stalk angle. He'll know
their insights if he can. A flower's mind
is well-aligned with his, holds perfect truths.

But reason has its limits. He can long,
at times, for colleagues on his summer strolls,
to vet ideas or just to socialize.
Small bees are peers he might consult; no fools,
they petal-hover in their counting, eyes
on primes. But they're aloof: he can't belong.

DISAGREEMENT IN ATHENS

I am a fragranter, a man who *maths*
the essence of how flowers verve the air
with scent on summer mornings. I divide
perfumes into a breeze; a cloud; sunsear.
My quotients clarify all fragrant truths;
establish formulae to further guide
me in analysis of subtleties
of sunsplash; bee love; slow and flowered breeze.

Sometimes I lecture on my niche in thought
to certain peers at the Academy.
Assert that I discern geometry
in slant of stalk, in how grand perfumes float
on whimsied air.

                    Not everyone agrees
that math is found in gardens; near by trees.

FRIENDS LEARN FROM EACH OTHER

My friend's a "calculator," fond of math,
like any old machine might tend to be.
Flowers to him are petal-numbers: no
attention paid to scent or beauty.

I, by contrast, am a fragranter,
a connossieur of perfumes on the path
through woods and fields each morning. What I know
includes some math. But other senses stir:

aroma love; bold sensuality;
deep passion that my younger friend can't feel
(though I don't mean he doesn't have a soul!)

We walk together, spy a chicory:
I twitch alert for scent. He rambles on
about prime-numbered petals, too soon gone.

LATE SUMMER

Butterflies lecture
on flutter with rapid wings.

Breezes learn quickly.

Bird, Flower, Waves

He's nicknamed colleagues in the art of math
his fellow "primers":

                      those who sequence well
the indivisible numbers that
are true immortals, irreversibly whole
as gods should be.

                  This morning on his path
atop a seaside cliff, he notices *two*:

a bluebird singing, full of lilt and wit,
and when her notes are counted:

                        Prime. Quite true
to their shared mind.

                The other: flower. Wise:
blue petal counts irregular and prime,
always.

        Both blue, just like the shimmering sea
that sunlight lathers. Waves curl into foam
at intervals:

      math students too.

Green Music

Such fog and dank are not unusual,
mid-spring, these parts.

                    Soon

noon sun caresses haze and gray to green:
deep glistening on the branches and leaves.

July may bake well-dry
but right now what a pleasure to
listen to the *drip-drip-drip*
of ever-shimmering morning dew.

Buzz On The Tenth Of August

A shortened month, three weeks left in it now.

Sunblaze begins to dwindle, subtly;

gnats are being woken by their clock
to congregate amidst the humid;

thicken blue wet air with hover,
whirl.

As you try to stand quite still,
and feel the earth rotating ever closer—
even sense its north/south axis leaning—
toward the not far off
chill of fall.

ICE AGE

You walk down the hot steps of August
into the black pool of autumn,
water much colder;

storms might erupt
with the suddenness of first frost.

Still, air's soft and hazy
this one afternoon
and you swim a few strokes
as if it's summer, just beginning,
and time still has
that endless feel.

The water's colder, sure,
but sunlight still can warm
the black mirror surface
of this glacier-scooped pool.

GLAZE

You walk down these shiny slate steps,
in late August's cooling fast stream—

slippery steps, smooth as glass—

into September's glaze.

Hot as summer but somehow different,
one yellow leaf striking you amidst green multitudes,
as if one sunray has soaked this leaf
amidst loud sweet waters.

AMUSEMENT PARK

August quite resembles
this swimming pool slide:
early on, midsummer's seethe
incites your downward arc
into splashing waters.

But later, now, a brisk of breeze
raises fleeting goose bumps
and you hesitate,
some silver clouds a warning.

The pool is much less crowded;
yet blue water beckons.
As you move down on your way,
you know that something's changed.

The Wright Brothers

If trees could fly:

                    leaves
would have to be their sleek wings.

Sad, flightless winters.

POLAR NATURE

Sublime and artful smoother of sharp rocks,
this stream has rounded stones ten million years;
observers in our town have written books,
in fact, on how the greatest sculptor is
pure icy water. August sunshine sears,
but glacial texture--polar nature--stays
embedded in its churn.

                              Exaggerate,
I might, about the books. But water's *cold*,
brrrish, first cousin to Antarctic ice.
I choose to emphasize its freeze, be bold,
dramatic even; Shakespeare wrote a poem
about this stream that runs right near our home,
a so small town. Too bad it's lost.

                                     Relate
the truth, and all you ever get are lies
hurled back at you. They love to criticize.
Say what you will, this world is not too nice.

THE CRAFT OF WATER AND LIGHT

It speaks a language for sure, this shallow stream
whose chief occupation appears to be
polishing stones so smoothly
they're almost jewels.

You listen intently to tinkle and bubble,
a cacophony of dash and splash,
a wavering rhythm of sound and motion,
fluctuation,
and couldn't be more certain
the stream is talking to you.
But oh to know what the words mean!

Perhaps if you were a bird,
or sun ray or overhanging branch,
translation might come more easily.

The pale brown stones the stream polishes
shimmer gemlike when a burst of sun,
parting-clouds emancipated,
catches them full.

Perhaps the stream, an artisan,
is speaking of the jeweled beauty
its own craft of water and light
creates.

You listen and listen until this language
tells you to move on.

THE RETURN

So slowly, sunlight warms the stream
this cold October morning.

Red and yellow leaves reflect
in stone-scooped pools where water rests
on its steep hill rush
toward the dark blue lake below.

A terrible wistfulness
encompasses you at how
ice will soon return again;

the same ice that gouged out
these leaf-reflecting pools
millennia ago.

CHAR

Evolution is time's sole master, yet

the day will come when the whole sun explodes,
earth's mere cinder and
chicories no longer will explain
prime numbers all day long to weeds and wind
through blue petal counts.

Sun worshippers are right.

Revel in the sizzling sky,
and savor every sun ray.

THE METAPHYSICS OF WEATHER

Amidst this freeze and stinging wind,
these tree-sourced squalls of snow
that only last a moment;

your challenge is to ponder
next June's dragonflies
gliding over their sun-lathered pond
as if there's only one season
and it is immortal;

as if this morning's Arctic purgatory
by then will be
long forgotten.

THE ACADEMY

Dragonfly zigzags,
amidst the slant of June rays,

teach geometry.

FREE OF CHARGE

In this locale of intense greenery—
at pond's edge—punctuated only by
widely spaced blue flowers,

you're struck by

how only blue or green late dragonflies
flit in the August sunshine, quite as if
efficient camoflauge determines tint,
even in this modest, tangled world.

You've seen them red and silver elsewhere, yes,
red orange as a sunset,
even white as snow,
but right here evolution's teaching
quite for free,
Selection's Seminar,
to you and ancient ferns,
and one quite gorgeous bee.

A Gust-Loved Leaf

One thousand million years ago,
plants gave away the right to walk
to a more frisky DNA
that cored the ant, the snail…
ourselves.

Tranquility proved tempting then,
though bark and thorns evolved like

skulls and fangs

for a safety minimum.

But *now* the yearning grows,
as nothing stays the same.
And you watch a gust-loved leaf
pinwheel across the road
and realize, how extraordinary
their road not taken.

The leaf spins higher into woods
where once upon a time
immobility seemed priceless,
motion just a waste of time.

First

Quite salamander-like, they made the trip
from shallow seas to land; to sunwarmed sand;
three hundred ninety million years ago.

First.

      One way? No!

               Theirs was a kind of loop
for several million years; a journey far more slow
than *Utah-by-mule-train* from way back when.

Niche creatures, they had eyes atop the head
to peer up, catch what water prey they could,
which made them come near land and bottom-crawl,
as if there was some plan to leave the sea.

Migration that would lead to you and me,
but actually...

           the "plan" was random genes,
and how their traits filled niches. Still, a thrill
to be the crawler who went *first* to see.

Of Mice And Time

(for Edna St. Vincent Millay's *Epitaph for the Race of Man*)

A hundred million years ago, and more,
the pterodactyls soared, and mammals dashed
and scurried: ancient shrews. Down on the floor
of giant forests, they could thrive. So fast,
they beat T-Rex's lunge, first birds' fierce dives.

Chaotic punctuation marks, they'd move
so randomly they managed to outlast
the dinosaurs. For when the meteor crashed
their burrows were secure, a year's gray sun
no problem for their scamper, flit and nest.
Another sixty million years, a blink
of time's expansive eye, a fleeting wink
for galaxies, black holes; and here we are:

noon rays emblazon this lush patch of grass;
an ancestor emerges on the run
from stray cat's stealthy stalk. No-one would guess
that mouse may be here long after we're gone.

A Certain Perspective

Now it's so quiet you can just about hear,
up on this winding, sun-warmed mountain road,
the whirring of electrons.

                                   Faintest buzz
inside the atoms in old massive trees
that line your way. So *quiet* here that you ponder
how in this stillest, deepest morning mood,
when you and oaks don't move, electrons race
in orbits in your atoms nonetheless.
Your flesh and elms' sunloving leafery
disguise the whirring emptiness within;
the world impersonates real substance with
the art of atom-shadow. Sorcery
we make a science of. An art so smooth,
no telling where it ends and life begins.

BLUE SKY BASK

You lean back at your desk,
gaze at the balmy blue
and know this could be
how it ends.

It doesn't feel *that* bad,
the idea of floating away
along with scattered atoms,
feeling something mysterious
and new;

a different kind of chilly,
darker than the absence of light
but not as cold as might
be expected.

SAVANTS

Late April's been as cold as early March
but gnats can wait no longer:

spring must be!

They whirl amidst surprising snowflakes;
buzz your nose;
and highlight primal chords
of briefly seething sunlight
across your startled vision.

Gnats are your favorite calendar-savants:

they banish winter where it really matters,
in your timedrenched thoughts.

This Puff Of Air

Flight is not the only gift:
there's *hover*, too.

Gnats stay aloft
near perfectly still,
resting on this puff of air or that.

Savants of June light, skillful as
the coasting hawks in their own way.

Behold:

they float just like the shimmering sun
in noon's deep sky,
sun not much more ancient than

they are.

CONCENTRICITIES

You see the world through eyes so tiny that
a leaf's an ocean; or, at least, a lake.

You are Sir Wing Flash, flitting royal gnat
and likely you will never write a book
or draw a sketch, or sing except for buzz,
but you're my hero, nonetheless.

                                   A breeze, a gust,
and now your whirl is gone; replaced
by empty sunlight. Here, amidst birch trees,
I ponder your quick-winged, spin legacy;
fine master of blue air, big crowd, flight pace.

I have a sense you know geometry!

Your concentricities in air amaze.

The Neurasthenic Oak Tree

My nerves must settle down
and soothe themselves.

The worst of winter's gone;
all my wiry branches will heal,
if only given a chance.

The sun is pleasantly ticklish
this morning;
it makes my far twigs sparkle
in the bright yellow buzz
of sky-climbing bees;

in the well-lit promise of April,
and June, its near and distant lover.

Trees By Ginger F. Zaimis

Trees:

what if,
we are the trees and they are us;
our siblings?

Branches as arms; feet for rooting.

Animated trunks—
Made from the same; inter-mingling.

Thrash And Ripple

For anyone who doubts the subtle math
of winter streams, stand here and ponder well
the *ratio*, black glinting flow to snow;

concentric scatter, light motes as they spill
atop fast water over rocks. The path
they take is rough geometry. Not slow,
but yet as if reflected on. Thoughtful.

You find intelligence in measured pace
of snowmelt flow, its downhill angle, foam.
Wood bridge you gaze from is quite peaceful but
there's wilder thrash and ripple here, below:
unruly math in charge as well, no doubt.

A paradox: strict rules that call for roam.

Such winter beauty, with math's subtle grace.

LAST FULL DAY, FIRST HALF OF

summer.

These human subdivisions
don't do justice to
the poignancy of how
this leaf, still fully green,
is severed by a gust
and flutters slowly downward,

as if a modest portent of
red-leaved decline, soon to come.

So Green

The faintest twang
from near the pond
marks the start
of summer love.

Mild bull-chord that,
soon enough,
will make the lilies tremble.

Morning's quiet, otherwise.

Profoundly green leaves
seem to quiver
at the slightest thought of love.

Midsummer Love

It's only early August but the frogs
are vanished now from their small oval pond.

No more bull chords vibrating like
the cellos of midsummer's lust.

Vanished for another year.

Makes you reflect on how inexorable
the orbiting of earth is.

Reflect in silence, on this sunscorched road,
where recently love twanged.

That Brief

That June was like a port of refuge. Slow
as an hourglass. Molasses. Slow as the Bay of Naples
we gazed at for long hours, *largesse* but
with limits sharper than we could have known.
Nothing we could say
would make July 1st tickets go away.
We tried to give departure not a thought
and watched how breezes made the sailboats sway,
the gulls flutter. The *linger* in a kiss
made twilight pause and moonrise hesitate
and nothing for it, then, but to stay calm,
wait until reunion in the fall.

That brief.

Samos: Looking Back From Athens

It's funny what associations last,
and bridge the gulf of years. *That lemonade
a vendor used to hawk,* as aromatic as
a sunwashed grove. We passed him daily on our walks:
beyond the road, blue shimmer of the bay.

In bed by noon, the afternoon a swoon
of love, heat-drained fatigue, then rootlessness.
There is no wandering like that of youth.

Awakening at 5 PM, the terrace next—
iced tea with lemon as the sun declined—
the future vague as filmy dusk's descent,
its early stars bejeweling sky and sea.

Now hint of lemon on this sudden breeze
from who knows where, quite like a sorcerer's:

it conjures *you* at peaceful Strefi Hill:
almost that swoon. Almost that morning walk.

STILL

Cicadashrill smoothes into autumn's Slow
while leaves that dry and start to tatter

sing,

in high pitched crackle.

Breeze-strummed melodies
of taut decline
amidst the deepening chills.

Full orchestra of snow
is just now warming up.

Still, cicadas sing.

THE INFINITE

Her gift is in sheer artistry of *shrill*,
a fluent flutery, creative lilt.
No nearby bird is like her, can command
such fluid repertoire of warbling sound,
notesong. The beauty makes you stand and listen, still
as any oak: the last time that you felt
such inspiration was in early youth.
First Mozart, maybe? Even that did not
quite penetrate like this performance. Leaves;
blue brook; are speaking their midsummer truth,
their shimmering and bubbling froth, through her!
Her sunwashed notes make something start to stir
within not felt before. Her deep song thieves
your Reason, leaves you with the infinite.

BIRD IN THE LOW LYING BRANCHES

Pressure and stress,
a hybrid called *stressure*,
he can alleviate
by looking long at this fast flowing stream;
the wakes of white foam jutting stones create.

With an autumn sense that soon
ice will start to *imperial*
the surface of flashing water.

His burden is the long flight south
just around the corner.

For now asymmetry
of water's spray and jumble, tumble and flash
bestows a kind of placidity,
easing stressure's gnaw-saw.

Each Cell Has Its Own Clock

Immortal leaves sprout in these maple woods:
they turn each fall to yellow, red and bronze
but never wither, crackle, fall to the ground.

Turn green again, late March. You noticed this
when you were young, but never thought it through
and now, old aged, you walk here all the time
and wonder if next spring just might
gloss your hair all black again, one hour, one day.

You've never shared these woods with anyone
so no-one can be with you, then, to glimpse
such a youthful turn. But radiant trees themselves could share
your sway in time.

            Some freakish backwards clock
that ticks inside of cells, keeps these leaves young,
and flames a tree crown *rainbow*, this pale noon
in mid-November, as some chill gusts swirl.

CHILL

I am the leader of the pack. On this,
the thirty-first of August, I have turned
a shade of royal scarlet. *All around,*
my followers stay green. Cicada-sound,
gray clouds and cooling breeze start to confirm
my standout color is near punctual.
And yet it shocks with its dramatic splash,
connoting blood that sunrays quietly wash.

My green flock sways, regarding me with awe—
my scarlet shimmer, truth amidst this balm—
for soon the yellow orange swoon of fall
will dapple all these woods while chill descends.

I am the leader of the pack and all
keep careful eye on my blood tint. My clock.

As The Year Turns: After L. Zukofsky

A weak *cicadashrill* persists until
the trees are ravaged bare by chill and gusts
that howl that soon,
December will arrive.

It all seems usual and yet you stand

                                              quite still,

delighted by a chicory! She *lasts*,
despite earth's tilt away from sunlight's soothe,
in bluish purple radiance. You live
year round for such robust anomalies--

impossible ice-sliver in the pond
in July's seethe;
a tuft of warmth in February's freeze--

there's no excluding chance from inexorable fate;
no formula for *All*.

                            "The green leaf that
outlasts the winter" speaks of error's hope,
just like a dragonfly's midwinter loop.

Symphonic

Cicadashrill envelops August late,
a kind of whistling rising up to greet
the seethe and sear of 10 AM:

midair above the deep green woods.

Shrill whistling with a beauty that's
symphonic, poignant,

languaging

the imminence of fall.

RANDALL JARRELL'S PIECE OF SUN

All sunlight's flush against this hill, one hour
past rosy dawn: his favorite moment in
his morning walk. Bright sunshine conjures hopes
as do a warbler's notes, a swallow's loops.
The news, as usual, brought swirling fear,
but that's humanity. He loves the sun:
it spawned all life and fueled four billion years
of crawl and flight, scatter, elation; ruin
for individuals and species.

                      Time's
implacable and angry like some god
mythology created; but light's real,
a balm for billions, spark; and splashy rhymes
to satisfy a free verse poet. Brood
on war and famine, yes. But sun prevails.

"THE DEAD" BY JAMES JOYCE

Hard slant of light, mid-February. Cold.
But snow gleams brightly in this winter wood,
as if the snow itself cannot grow old.
Hard slant of light, mid-February. Cold.
Young Michael Furey's love was just too wild
for our denying world: on this you brood.
Hard slant of light, mid-February. Cold.
But snow gleams brightly in the winter wood.

Himalayan Whales

Above the Adirondacks looking west, piled high,
immense white clouds like brand new mountains: bright
in dawn's rose glow. *New* Himalayas, vast
as those real ones back in Nepal.

                              These'll last,
you dream; just like geology. And yet
already winds fray certain peaks. You sigh
at all of nature's frailness, brevity.

The Himalayas rose from a shallow sea
where whales had evolved: what irony, such change,
catalyzed by gleaming rock, vast size.

Enormous earth itself can rearrange
its own robust details, in time.

                              It's wise
for us to see the transitory:

cloud-mountains tell fragility's true story.

PALEONTOLOGISTS' VACATION

The old stone house had a wooden pier
that jutted out right from the porch;

                             down steps;
then out ten yards above clear deep Long Lake.

We'd laze there August mornings; tan; and look
at blue-white dragonflies' quick gleaming loops.
Hot summer dwindling; still, without a care
as if each morning was immortal.

                            Now,
we knew the dragonflies would not live long
as individuals, but could respect
three hundred million years.

                      Long Lake allowed
perspective on grand solstice time:

                        belong
to this species or that, the brevity
of summer—*all seasons*--shadows revelry.

But we took refuge in what could distract:
a cloud's reflection, water's mirroring trick.

A Feast For All

A dinosaur's last meal was fossilized,
one hundred million years ago. *Some twigs
and berries, ferns*: all vegetarian.

No T-Rex here: well-lived benevolence;
a giant stalking greenery in bogs,
dense swamps. More study needed now, but a sense
already of fine dining. No matter wind,
or rain; fierce heat;

                 and further thoughts arise
of calories and size. Of exercise;
metabolism; musclemass.

                   Let's not,
however, wreck all awe with modern facts.
Time has performed a startling, wondrous trick:
we've traveled back! And now let's sit and eat
quite luscious ferns. This swamp's gourmet surprise.

SUNRED SPLASH

I saw the brontosaurus head upstream;
so briefly, just a flicker of a view:
dark brown, blunt-jawed, long-necked.

                                       I swear, it's true!

And then, it plunged. And life became the same
again; two hundred million years: one flash.

The mind can travel just like so, but this
was real. A dino-child, perhaps. Its *Is,*
despite extinction, made a sunred splash
in all the murky entrails of my mind.

I wish for it to come once more. Instead,
the stream now shows just dawn.

                               Sure, I could read
of dinosaurs. Unlikely, though, to find
one in the flesh again. The worth
of such a moment's infinite. *Time's truth.*

Before The Lisbon Earthquake

In the days before the Lisbon Earthquake,
many warnings were given:
Birds were heard speaking in tongues.
Children spat up blood as they dreamed of ruins.
Along the coast not so far away,
waves turned crimson at nightfall.
Moonlight mixed with their rosy glow
to create pink, blood-like shadows.
But no-one paid attention.

In an asylum a madman dreamed
the entire event in vivid detail.
Because he claimed God gave him the news
he was ignored, then threatened.

Most telling of all were the stones:
ordinary rocks, paving blocks, throughout the streets,
and boulders on the outskirts of town:
all cracked in spectacular sequence,
new lines and fissures appearing at once,
forming letters in every known language,
spelling out imminent doom.

Some rocks even duplicated what was coming,
splitting to bits without ready cause,
imitating earthquake's pure chaos,
the ground's disobedience to its own strength.
No-one read the ground beneath them at all
except for an old woman named Isabel Lopes,
who heard birds' warnings and read rocks' letters.
Her recognition was deemed so outlandish
that her family hid her in their cellar
where she was one of the first to die.

One mini-whirlwind of sapphire light
went so far as to warn an eight year old boy
darting through alleyway shadows
looking for fruit rolled off a wagon.
Like the rest of the city, his family did not believe
because they'd never heard of a prophet
come as a wave, a rock, a bird,
or an amorphous being bathed in blue light—
not as a statue in some church alcove.

On the day the earthquake came,
there was no warning at all.

Before The Lisbon Earthquake
Translated Into Greek By Stamatis Polenakis

ΠΡΙΝ ΤΟΝ ΣΕΙΣΜΟ ΤΗΣ ΛΙΣΣΑΒΩΝΑΣ

Πριν τον σεισμό της Λισσαβώνας, τις μέρες που προηγήθηκαν
ακούστηκαν πολλές προειδοποιήσεις:
τα πουλιά τραγουδούσαν όλα μαζί στις ακατάληπτες γλώσσες τους,
παιδιά έφτυναν αίμα και έβλεπαν στα όνειρά τους ερείπια.
Όχι μακριά, κατά μήκος της ακτής,
το κατακόκκινο δείλι βυθιζόταν μέσα στη θάλασσα,
το φως του φεγγαριού διαλυόταν μέσα στην πορφυρή ανταύγεια των κυμάτων
ρίχνοντας βαριές σκιές αίματος αλλά κανείς δεν έδινε σημασία.

Σ` ένα άσυλο, ένας τρελός ονειρεύτηκε
με κάθε λεπτομέρεια τα επερχόμενα
αλλά επειδή μιλούσε για κάποιο μήνυμα σταλμένο απ` τον Θεό
στην αρχή τον αγνόησαν και μετά τον απείλησαν.

Πιο καθαρά απ` όλους μίλησαν οι πέτρες
οι βράχοι, τα πλακόστρωτα στη μέση των δρόμων
οι μεγάλες λίθινες πλάκες στα περίχωρα της πόλης
άρχισαν όλες να σπάζουν μ` έναν εκκωφαντικό θόρυβο
ξεχύνοντας από μέσα τους αλλόκοτα σχήματα και μορφές
λέξεις γραμμένες σ` όλες τις γνωστές γλώσσες
που μιλούσαν για την μελλοντική συμφορά.

Κάποιο βράχοι άρχισαν να σχίζονται ανεξήγητα σεκομμάτια
μιμούμενοι το απόλυτο χάος του σεισμού
την ανυπακοή της γης στην ίδια τη δύναμή της.
Κανείς δεν διάβασε τους οιωνούς και τα σημεία
εκτός από μια γριά με τ` όνομα Ιζαμπέλ Λόπες
που άκουσε τις φωνές των πουλιών και διάβασε
τις λέξεις πάνω στις πέτρες

αλλά όσα έλεγε ήσαν τόσο αλλόκοτα
που οι δικοί της την κλείδωσαν στο υπόγειο
κι εκεί τη βρήκε πρώτη απ᾽ όλους, ο θάνατος.

Ένας μικρός ανεμοστρόβιλος από γαλάζιο φως
ήρθε για να προειδοποιήσει ένα οκτάχρονο αγοράκι
που τριγύριζε στα σκοτεινά σοκάκια
μαζεύοντας τα φρούτα που έπεφταν απ᾽ τις άμαξες
Όπως όλοι οι άλλοι στην πόλη, η οικογένειά του
δεν κατάλαβε τίποτα
γιατί ποιος άκουσε για τον ερχομό ενός προφήτη
με τη μορφή ενός κύματος, μιας πέτρας, ενός πουλιού
ή ενός χωρίς μορφή πλάσματος που έρχεται πλημμυρισμένο
σε γαλανό φως-
κι όχι σαν άγαλμα σε προαύλιο εκκλησίας
Τη μέρα που έφθασε ο σεισμός
δεν υπήρξε ούτε μια προειδοποίηση.

Macbeth's Castle: Philosophers' Woods

We slowly make out ramparts in the gloom
as we approach, traversing muddy woods
and windstrewn bramble from the recent storm.

The castle is a ruin and yet walls seem
as "solid" as Prince Hamlet's flesh; rank weeds
are everywhere, but towers still have form
aloft:

        while yellow pennants flutter high
against a foggy, gust-twirled sky.

We stride no more, unnerved; observe a face
quite fleeting in a window. Pale, austere;
perhaps she isn't pleased by our approach.

We'd seen a photo; wreckage should be near
and not this trembling, full blown relic;

                                      such
is reason's endless instability
that when her face returns we turn and flee.

Deep Scottish truth seems well beyond our reach,
obscured by shadows we can never breach.

Empty Glory

This drear and mist, and soggy breeze,
announce September in
these lush and tangled emerald woods
that soon enough will be less green,
and punctuate high leafery
with yellow, splashing leaves.

His castle is not far away
and you anticipate he might appear
at any moment, stepping out
from right behind a venerable tree,

attire soaked in blood.

But all you see are strands of fog
wrapped around moss-covered trunks,
as if embracing ancient loves,
in all the full desire of ghosts.

"Macbeth, Macbeth, where are you,
still demented with ambition
after centuries of sleep?"

Blank chilly fog is silent as
a looming sense of autumn
embedded in a sudden, northern gust;
now all you're left with are reflections:

bloody dagger, furrowed brow;
his realization that
fiendish fate has tricked him
into empty glory
so very long ago.

SILENT CAL IN THE WOODS

In 1926, my father, age 13, shook hands with President Calvin Coolidge in the White House, then open to the public on Thursdays.

This cardinal is the President of Chill,
red jauntiness amidst ice-jangling trees,
displaying leadership, red-feathered will,
no matter wintry gusts. Beloved by
electorate of deer, staunch oaks, south breeze--
such loyalists to warmth--it's quite clear why
December voters stay steadfast.

                           She wins
despite the enmity of flailing snow;
the bitter ice of streams. Parade's right now,
redflit exciting leafless branches so
their clatter turns applause. Redstreak allows
the gauntest oaks hot dreams of summer suns.

Her simple style evokes our "Silent Cal":
no lengthy speeches. Redhop rules over all.

Snowfall Always Fit By Robert Basner

First Snowfall

*i.m. Marie Ponsot, who reminisced that, while she
had spent many summers on the farm, she had never
stayed through to winter*

First snowfall always fit,
Fall brought to being's bare.
Thaw the sweet of it.

Pine urges earth in it,
Green's coldest color; there
First snowfall always fit.

Like leaf, the fall of it,
How full is fragmenter;
Thaw the sweet of it.

Falls other falls in it,
As this is ancient air:
First snowfall always fit.

One landscape leaves in it,
One withers in its own year,
Thaw the sweet of it.

Leaving always fit,
Though summer itself were there.
First snowfall always fit:
Thaw the sweet of it.

Pythagoras, Revolutionary

Two hundred years he's been a sprawling oak;

his favorite time of year lush summer; (now
it's August, leaves as bright as gemlike sky).

Before oak, swift, who loved to coast and look
down through the tangled crowns of trees. Allow
herself the luxury of glide: but sigh,
sometimes, at summer's brevity. And then...

brief glimpses of lives further back. Dream-like.
His favorite (the most human) glistening view
of oar handle in oarlock: rough seas-sprayed,
though sunjeweled too, and polished by the wind.

How poignant to have been a galley slave:
one of a nameless, mercilessly beaten crew.
Then *freed* by shipwreck: to begin, again.

Ancestors

A squirrel's jaunty bounce across the road
suggests real *personality*. Perhaps
she was a frisky monkey lives before;
or it's bright dawn that's made her spirits soar.

Ebullience in a swift's blue sunwashed loops,
could well be either too: past life

                                        or verve,
arising from the sparkle bright sun's made
and showered on each quick-winged swoop and swerve.

He can't remember his own previous
existences, though many later claim
he could. However, he detects such heritage
in others readily enough;

                              in life
such faith is more steadfast for him than proof.
Both squirrel, swift perhaps were once a sage.

His story's blurred *before* Pythagoras,
but each ancestor's treasured all the same.

LOGICIAN OF THE LEAVES

He's always had two separate tendencies:
the mystical; the mathematical.

They now emerge anew with *leafery;*
initially he's sought out prophecy,
leaves' dangles, angles, shapes as oracles.
But, nothing works.

                But now there's April's breeze,
and how its ripples change leaf-patterns so:
a calculus. Math's challenge for Pythagoras,
to summon theorems from his abacus;
interpret what spring's leaves and breeze may know.

Leaf-shadows in late morning can enhance
precision in his gaze; like second looks
at shift and blur. At sway.

                 And best he takes
logic *alone* from breeze and leaves' bright dance.

GREEN

His brightest pupil is Mathimatikos;
Samoan like himself; a prince. Who grasps
equations in an instant like a hawk
sees vectors for new flight. A swallow, loops.
And yet he is reflective on a walk,
or sitting watching waves along the coast;
he's searching for a grander theorem than
mere ratio.

       A theorem for this green:
wet April woods, moss on a streamwashed stone,
a perfect leaf. An iridescent bug.

And *no real gap* between branches, his bones,
between his mind or body and a log.
A world of One—divide it up—but still,
it always seems to add up to a Whole.

In A Pond

Concentricity
of raindrops' April ripples
teaches math to clouds.

CHALLENGE OF THE WIND

A steady rain gives opportunity
to teach a class in concentricity.

He wanders to a stream where splashing drops
create relentless circle-ripples that
display geometry; fine math and wit
regarding curves and space.

                        No swallow's loops
show greater skill than water in true form.

His nearby pupils focus on his words
of explanation. But when fresh wind stirs
the raindrops' perfect circles elongate;
distort; in ways he cannot calculate.

Some pupils grow confused; flutter their wings;
or even fly away. He hesitates:
he can't make sense of windsmeared water rings.

THE ATHENS ACADEMY

Reluctantly, at last, he will inquire
if he can lecture once again (for free)
at the Academy.

              He'll need release,
at least briefly, from exile. Have to see
about a pardon, even. Maybe face
some ancient enemies.

                 But colleagues here—
confined to birds and breeze—just can't fulfill
the need for colloquy to make thoughts whole.

He has progressed in reading *leafery*,
a secret language that he longs to share
with peers; as in his long gone, august past.

It's only intellect that brings him peace.

He'll send the letter soon. He must not fear
his own afflicted history.

              Must try to trust the scholarly.

A Beach In Samos: Quiet Light

This late life opportunity astounds,
although he's known for months it could occur:
a year's release to lecture once again,
on *leafery*, at the Academy.

While in Athens he finds a boat; a steady wind
is favorable to reaching his old shore.
This morning he begins to make the rounds
of boyhood haunts: a rough biography
of how his deepest vision came to be.

These gulls that glide and swerve adroitly were
the earliest to teach him math of flight.
Remain his sunwashed, surf-commanding peers.

He's not too old to wonder how sunlight
has learned so many angles perfectly.

ANTIDOTE

These gulls must be descendants of savants
he met in childhood, and who tutored him
in math: what he could fathom of it, then.

One glide, two swerves; dividing salt-tanged wind
so they can coast and perch. He stares at them,
at beakshape, wingfluff, any resemblance
that might inspire recognition. Eyes
that flicker meeting his as if aware,
remarkably, of family history.

But looks are blank. No wings that beat in sudden surprise.
And yet he loves the sense of harmony
between first years and last. Deep bond, right here.

Metapontum's antidote: Samos;
this beach whose gulls well taught Pythagoras.

CYCLES IN SAMOS

The time between all waves is like a clock
that also measures quiet, poise.

                              Irregular,
it's true, for no two lulls are quite the same,
but rhythmic; and, somehow, pause reassures
Pythagoras of calm amidst wild spray,
gulls wheeling, sunlight gleaming.

                              He can take
a theorem, he is sure, from ratios
between wave crumbles and the intervals
that follow sleekly. Or, divide a breeze
by seagull's swerve to understand her flight.
Work hard.

              But now the cresting rhythm lulls
him into *ponder.* Merging with slow light.
He's of this surf, he speculates; *from* wind.

Soon after crests crash down, new waves begin.

Field Trips, Athens, 202 B. C.

He tells his students to range far and wide,
and find examples of a natural math
that's "comparable" to humans'. In a week,
they will discuss:

                    "I have observed the tide,
precise in its progressions."

                          "I've found truth
about prime numbers with the chicory;
its petal-counts' blue patterns."

                              "Raindrops; leaves;
a ratio's accessible if you
are patient."

                      "Also one between the dew
and dawn's first rays."

                          The last to speak:
"I simply sat and watched how sunlight moves
across my garden. Such geometry
compares to Euclid's. I cannot decide
which one's superior. Depends on my mood."

TRIP TO PAROS: UNDERWATER

Byron's graffiti

glimmering on the seawall

at a shallow depth.

Macbeth's Castle

These woods obscure our distant Scottish view,
the River Tay not far away. Macbeth's
old castle now a ruin: sunsoaked dense pines
make inaccessible the sparse stone lines
where massive walls once stood. Abode of wrath—
ambition—blood. *The Lady would pursue*
a glory quickly dust.

              You ponder fate:
mere chance or character's sure destiny?
The answer may lie past this tangled wood;
so on you trudge and as you go you brood
on how a sense of deep philosophy
imbues these trees. Will Shakespeare may have felt
this mood, and maybe Hume. You see the ruin
much better now; and will be near it soon.

Italian Spring

A Roman Senator, now lost to time:
one Julius Aurelius *intrigues*
this rainy afternoon; as water slants
against Library windows.

                               Fragments can't
complete his portrait but you start to see
one aspect of his personality:
in any situation he would gauge
emotions on a scale. Faith in math his theme.

Yes, inner life all measure: one to ten,
no matter grief or laughter, passion too;
he numbered even love!

                          Or so this poet says.
The rain lets up; the murmur of a breeze
moves bright green leaves. *You dream his life back then.*

A certain urge to order things comes through.

EXCHANGE STUDENTS

after "The Sycamores of Rome" by Carol Goodman

Library.

Sunlight slanting in
the open window; pooling on
the nestled head of one young scholar
cradled,
sleeping hard at noon.

The Rome of revelry and riot, just the other night,
now sleeps the ancient sleep
of memory and fog.
A breeze riffles the open pages of

Horace.

A pair of readers now,
one much more attentive than
the other.

THE SYCAMORES OF ROME BY CAROL GOODMAN

These sycamores' bark peels
in the delicate shades
of quattrocentro fresco.
One tree's trunk is as pale as honeydew rind
scraped in places to reveal
the watery green fruit inside.

They remind you of the sycamores
in Rome and how their leaves
swirled in the dusk bright Tiber
and papered the rain corroded haunches
of Garibaldi's horse in the park
at the top of the Janiculum
where women, still soft eyed
from siesta, strolled arm-in-arm
above the many breasted city.

You could compare the color of their leaves
to the bricks that wall the road
uncoiling down the hill, or the rust dusting
slim hips of boys tilting backwards in fountains,
but what you remember
is a single arrow of sun
shooting through Latin class
to strike the studiously bent head
of your fellow scholar,
setting dull brown hair into flames of Titian red,
so that you stumbled over your Virgil translation
losing the measure of your own heart's beat.

The next day you crested the hill
on your way to mail a letter at the Vatican

and found the bronze clad
sky had split open to let in
the Appenines standing sentinel
above the winter besieged city.

On your last morning you went
back to the park on top of the hill,
but weather had already done what
failing memory never would:
wound the thick white wool
of fog, like a sheet tangled
in sleep-sprawled limbs,
around the achingly fine bones
of your lost beloved city.

Window In Medical School, Bologna, 1306

The lecturer drones on: loud, tedious.
Minutae on "the humors." Worthless lies.
He focuses instead on sunlight's creep
across the street. As if Pythagoras,
assessing rays' bright angles; sunlight's wise,
unlike this "teacher." Humors: blah! He'd mope
without light's angles to examine, count,
predict the pace of sun's bright sky-speed from.

His foolish parents sent him here instead
of hiring math's best tutor. No, he can't
engage with doltish rants! His love's for sum
and quotient, theorem.

                    Rather than just brood,
he lets the street and sunlight teach. No way
he'll let his parents waste another day.

THE PATIENT IS THE WIND

Most trees do not attend a medical school,
and never swear the Hippocratic Oath.

But every May they are medicinal.

Most trees do not attend a medical school,
but practice *leafery* which makes air whole;
they swear allegiance to green's endless truth.

Most trees do not attend a medical school,
and never swear the Hippocratic Oath.

WITHOUT WANDERLUST

I am a rock; I have not moved
in sixteen thousand years.
My life is slow, the cave quiet:

I never shed tears.

There was a time—the glacier trudged—
I took its massive ride,
but sunlight came and then the melt—
I tumbled into this cave—
wild plummet, *roar,* as if riding
a giant cracked-ice wave.

My memories are just this one,
as if my life began
at Ice Age end
in melt and scour that scooped
so many hills and gullies from
broad earth's relentless plain.

Yet I'm far *older* than that, so I'm told
by lichens on my skin
who miss bright sun in shadow here
but *green* on anyway.

I'd like some memories of those lost days
lichens *rumor*: days of rain, sunsear.
But failing them, I savor tufts
of breeze at early dusk,

and revel in my stillness (opposite
to strivers' wanderlust).

Acknowledgments

Much gratitude to the editors of the following journals in which some of these poems first appeared, sometimes under different titles or in slightly different form: *Anemone* (US) and *Agenda* (UK) ("Before the Lisbon Earthquake"), *Blueline* ("Last Full Day, First Half Of," "Painting In the High Peaks," "Painting near Blue Mountain," "Paleontologists' Vacation," "Savants," and "Vermeer Near Tupper Lake"), *Green Hills Literary Lantern* ("The Craft of Water and Light"), and *Millers Pond Poetry Magazine* ("Himalayan Whales").

As usual a comprehensive list of those to whom I am indebted is too long for print, but I would like to first of all thank M. Ann Petrie, my most encouraging, inspirational and insightful writing teacher at CCNY back in 1971-72. My other brilliant teachers (of fiction, literature and astronomy as well as poetry) to whom I am grateful include William Gaddis, Howard Bernstein, Anthony Burgess, Adrienne Rich, Kurt Vonnegut Jr., Harry Steven Lazerus and William Matthews at CCNY; Daniel Hoffman, David DeLaura, Jim Rosier and Bob Perelman at the University of Pennsylvania; and A. E. Stallings at the Athens Centre in Greece, where Director Rosemary Donnelly has been a source of tremendous support over the years.

My encouraging and inspirational "working writer" colleagues often contributed inimitable work and/or commentary to this volume: Dr. Robert C. Basner, Stu Bartow, Carol Goodman, Katherine Hastings, Sharon Israel, Harry Steven Lazerus, Stamatis Polenakis, Nora Slonimsky, Tim Suermondt, Barbara Ungar, Pui Ying Wong, and Ginger F. Zaimis, along with those in "The Poetry Annex": Dr. Robert C. Basner, Elizabeth J. Coleman, and Licia Hahn. My editor and publisher at Spuyten Duyvil Press, Tod Thilleman, has provided crucial support and encouragement for a decade now. And, so many others whom I already regret not mentioning!

Lee Slonimsky has published ten collections of poetry. His third book, *Pythagoras in Love*, has been translated into French by the poet Elizabeth J. Coleman, and is currently being translated into modern Greek by the poet Stamatis Polenakis. With his wife, Hammett and Mary Higgins Clark Award winning novelist Carol Goodman, Lee has co-authored the *Black Swan Rising* trilogy. Lee is also a hedge fund manager who invests on behalf of the welfare and humane treatment of animals.